SAMUEL BUTLER
ON THE
RESURRECTION

SAMUEL BUTLER ON THE RESURRECTION

Edited and introduced by
Robert Johnstone

with an Appendix by
W.B. Primrose

COLIN SMYTHE
Gerrards Cross, 1980

Introduction © 1980 by Robert Johnstone
Appendix II © 1980 by W.B. Primrose

This edition first published in 1980 by Colin Smythe Ltd.,
P.O. Box 6, Gerrards Cross, Buckinghamshire

British Library Cataloguing in Publication Data

Butler, Samuel, *b. 1835*
The evidence for the resurrection of Jesus
Christ. Samuel Butler on the resurrection.
1. Jesus Christ – Resurrection – Biblical teaching
2. Bible. New Testament. Gospels – Criticism, interpretation, etc.
I. Title   II. Johnstone, Robert, *b. 1900*
232.9'7   BT481

ISBN 0-901072-59-1

Distributed in N. America by Humanities Press Inc.
171 First Avenue Atlantic Highlands,
N.J. 07716

Printed in Great Britain
Typeset by Inforum Ltd., Portsmouth
and printed and bound by Billing & Sons Ltd
Guildford, London & Worcester

Contents

Introduction

When Christianity was young it was the miraculous element in the Gospel story that attracted converts and sustained their faith under persecution. Today this same miraculous element drives people away from Christianity by requiring Christians to profess historical beliefs which are felt to be an affront to reason. Yet those who still believe in Christian values, of which truth is one, cannot afford to disregard the miracles; they are embedded in the faith and have to be accounted for.

The archetypal Christian miracle is the Resurrection, the raising of Jesus from the dead, and it is on this that the sceptics have chiefly concentrated. Some maintain that the historical evidence is too slender, was recorded too long after the event, and has been too heavily tampered with for any conclusions to be reached on the circumstances of the crucifixion, or even on whether it took place at all. According to the Jewish Talmud, Jesus was executed by stoning and not crucifying[1]. Others are prepared to accept that Jesus died on the cross, but attribute his subsequent appearances to hallucinations on the part of his followers. There is, however, another and more startling theory, namely, that Jesus was not dead when his body was taken down from the cross, that he revived under the care of Joseph of Arimathea and did indeed reappear to his amazed disciples in the flesh. The most convincing advocate of this last theory is Samuel Butler, but owing to the manner of its presentation his analysis of the evidence has been ignored for more than a century. In the more liberal climate of opinion today it deserves to be considered.

Samuel Butler, who lived from 1835 to 1902, is an author whose stature increases with the years. Dismissed during his lifetime as a minor literary figure and something of a crank, he has recently been described by Sir Karl Popper as 'one of the greatest of English philosophers'[2]. This is high praise from one of today's great philosophers, and it suggests that even Butler's lesser-known works should be treated with respect. One of these was an early pamphlet on the evidence for the Resurrection. Samuel Butler had had a strictly religious upbringing and his father intended him for the church; but after graduating at Cambridge he developed doubts about religion and declined to be ordained. In those days it was traditional for rebellious sons to be packed off to the colonies, and so young Butler was sent to New Zealand with sufficient capital to set up as a sheep farmer. In this he was so successful that after five years he had made enough money to enable him to retire. He sold up his farm, returned to England and lived thereafter in modest independence as an author, painter, musician and philosopher of common sense.

During the long, lonely evenings on his New Zealand farm Butler had undertaken a minute study of the four Gospels, which only served to confirm his religious doubts. By a painstaking process of comparison and deduction he reached, on purely internal evidence, the conclusion that has already been mentioned. In 1865, soon after his return to England, he published an anonymous pamphlet under the somewhat clumsy title: *The Evidence for the Resurrection of Jesus Christ as given by the Four Evangelists critically examined*. Butler sent a copy of this pamphlet to Charles Darwin, whom at that time he greatly admired. Darwin's letter of acknowledgement was cordial and approving: 'I am much obliged to you for so kindly sending me your *Evidence* etc. We have read it with great interest. It seems to me well written with much force, vigour and clearness: and the main argument is to me quite new. I particularly agree with all you say in your preface'[3].

In 1863, two years before the *Evidence*, the French scholar Ernest Renan had published his much-discussed *Vie de Jésus* which also plays down the miraculous element. It is rather surprising that he did not anticipate Butler's conclusion. Renan notes that the victims of crucifixion sometimes lived on for three or four days in atrocious agony, whereas Jesus is supposed to have died in a few hours. This blessed release Renan attributes to his 'delicate organization', although the biblical record of his travels and achievements suggest that Jesus must have been a person of exceptional stamina. Renan glosses over the central mystery of the Resurrection with a few perfunctory words about the strong imagination of Mary Magdalene. Butler does not mention Renan's book. He bases his own conclusion that Jesus survived crucifixion on four main considerations: 1. The period of actual crucifixion was relatively short, not more than six hours. 2. From the description, the spear wound does not appear to have been fatal or even serious. 3. The disciples were utterly unprepared for and amazed by the reappearance of Jesus, whereas a hallucination would suggest some previous expectation. 4. Nothing more is heard of Joseph of Arimathea, who should have been the principal witness of the Resurrection if it had occurred. Butler suggests that he knew otherwise but kept quiet for fear of punishment by the authorities. What happened in the end to Jesus we shall never know. He had powerful enemies who desired his death, and they would not be likely to fail a second time.

In spite of Darwin's approval the *Evidence* pamphlet was generally ignored and is now extremely rare. There is a copy in the British Museum of which the early part has been extensively revised in Butler's handwriting. Evidently he started to prepare a revised edition but abandoned it. In 1872 Butler published *Erewhon*, a satire on conventional religion, which was an immediate success; it was, in fact, the most successful book of his career. He then returned to the theme of the Resurrection and most unwisely decided to recast his theory in the form of another satire. Under the pseudonym of John Pickard Owen, a fictitious clergyman, Butler published *The Fair Haven* in 1873. This work purported to be a defence of Christian miracles by an orthodox theologian. In it Butler presented his own heretical conclusions in a highly convincing manner and pretended to refute them by the weakest of conventional arguments. The book was padded out by a discussion of other and less acceptable naturalistic explanations of the miracles, especially the hallucination theory of David Friedrich Strauss, a German theologian whose controversial *Leben Jesu* had been published in 1835. There was also a good deal of tongue-in-cheek moralizing and bogus theology, the whole preceded by a long posthumous memoir of the fictitious author by his equally fictitious brother. Altogether a most elaborate piece of humbug.

It seems that Butler expected *The Fair Haven* to be immediately recognized as a satire, but to his astonishment the book hoaxed nearly everybody. It was widely accepted as a serious defence of Christian orthodoxy, and one eminent divine even sent a copy to a friend who had religious doubts. The temptation to score off the Establishment was one which Butler could not resist. He quickly brought out a second edition under his own name with a preface which poked fun at his dupes. This literary escapade won him temporary notoriety at the cost of permanent eclipse. The serious and closely-reasoned argument which formed the core of the book could thereafter be dismissed as frivolous and unworthy of attention, and worse still, Butler's literary standing in other respects was permanently damaged. In the words of R.A. Streatfield, 'Reviewers fought shy of him for the rest of his life. They had been taken in once, and they took very good care that they should not be taken in again. The word went forth that Butler was not to be taken seriously, whatever he wrote, and the results of the decree were apparent in the conspiracy of silence that greeted not only his books on evolution, but his Homeric works, his writings on art, and his edition of Shakespeare's sonnets.'

As a literary tour-de-force *The Fair Haven* is still worth reading. Since the *Evidence* Butler had gained experience as a writer, and his restatement of the survival theory is more readable than in the original pamphlet. Nonetheless its satirical fancy-dress puts *The Fair Haven* out of court, and it is time that Butler's serious argument was made available for study in its original form. In the present edition the pamphlet of 1865 is reprinted in full and without comment.

To it is appended an article by a distinguished surgeon that appeared in the *Hibbert Journal* of 1949. The author of this article does not mention Butler, but on the medical evidence he concludes independently that Jesus might well have been alive when his body was delivered to Joseph of Arimathea. I am grateful to the Hibbert Trustees for permission to reprint the article in full.

This little-known work by Samuel Butler is republished as a contribution towards what one hopes will be the ultimate emergence of a single World Faith. One of the principal barriers between Christianity and other religions is the Christian claim to a unique status for Jesus as the miraculous God-man who rose from the dead. Today it is not only the irreligious who jib at miracles; practising Christians have told me that they would be happier in their faith if they were not required to believe in physical impossibilities, but could follow Jesus simply as an inspired prophet in something like the way that Muslims follow Muhammad. Butler himself to the end of his life claimed to be a Christian although he rejected the Christian miracles. The following passage from one of his essays sums up his faith: 'The essence of Christianity lies neither in dogma nor yet in an abnormally holy life, but in faith in an unseen world, in doing one's duty, in speaking the truth, in finding the true life rather in others than in oneself, and in the certain hope that he who loses his life on these behalfs finds more than he has lost. What can Agnosticism do against such a Christianity as this? I should be shocked if anything I had ever written or shall ever write should seem to make light of these things'[4].

R.J.

REFERENCES

1. Arnold Toynbee, *A Study of History* Volume XII (O.U.P. 1961) p. 481
2. K.R. Popper, *Objective Knowledge* (O.U.P. 1972) p. 238.
3. Henry Festing Jones, *Samuel Butler, author of Erewhon, a Memoir* (Macmillan 1920) p. 117.
4. Samuel Butler, *Selected Essays* (Jonathan Cape, Travellers' Library 1927) p. 176. The passage occurs somewhat incongruously in an essay entitled *A Medieval Girl School*.

THE EVIDENCE

FOR

THE RESURRECTION

OF

JESUS CHRIST

AS GIVEN BY THE FOUR EVANGELISTS

CRITICALLY EXAMINED

LONDON
1865.

Preface

I HAVE no doubt that the line of argument taken in the following pages is a very old one, and familiar to all who have extended their reading on the subject of Christianity beyond the common English books. I do not wish to lay claim to any originality whatsoever. I can honestly say that all which I have here written has been thought out independently, but hundreds must have thought out, and many probably said, the same before me. I may be asked then, why I have printed my MS. at all? I would answer because I know of no English work in which my remarks were embodied, and because I am sure that comparatively few even among educated Englishmen are aware how conflicting the accounts of the resurrection are, or how easily they afford their own explanation if they are at all closely examined. I have asked people over and over again to tell me the difference between St. Matthew's account of the resurrection and St. John's: they could not do it without the book. Clergymen are just as ignorant upon the subject as laymen. I generally endeavour accidentally to ascertain from any clergyman, whether he has a distinct conception of the circumstances of the resurrection: the result I have found to be so uniform as to assure me that I am quite justified in printing the following pages, whether they be old or no. I am indeed very sorry to say that I know no German, and have never read one of the German rationalistic books, but I am told that my argument is only a portion of what we have in Strauss and Bauer, and many others. I have no doubt of it; neither do I doubt that they have said all that I have said much better than I can say it;

but I have flattered myself that by taking a single point – the strongest and best attested point – the very key stone of the whole system – and rivetting the attention of the reader to that only, I have given him as it were the kernel of all that need be said upon the matter, the rest suggesting itself obviously without further adnotation. My chief regret is that no publisher of position will publish heresy so rank as mine; no matter how temperate the tone, or how honest the intention of the writer, unless I were a bishop, or at least an archdeacon, no publisher would take my MS. I cannot wonder at *them*: but I stand perfectly amazed at the intellectual cowardice with which we English – the physically bravest people on the face of the earth – refuse to allow of discussion upon the most important of all subjects. That we shall do ourselves some permanent mischief if we continue so intolerant of the fair exercise of the reason I am very sure: no nation can stand such a want of intellectual *morale* in the nineteenth century: I trust and think that it has its root in a good quality, and that when the time comes for it to pass away, pass it will; but at present it is very bad. It stands just thus. A man has remarks to make on certain discrepancies of the four evangelists, remarks which must occur to any one who has tried to put the four narratives together, and which, even if they be erroneous, should be published in order that their error may be publicly exposed, instead of being latently held by hundreds: and yet no publisher of position can make them public, even if he would, without doing himself a greater injury than he would be warranted in doing. The public are are to blame and not the publisher, but surely it is no small cause for wonder that a man should be unable to publish even at his own risk, doubts which must be so very apparent to so very many.

Since the above was sent to press I have been led to change my opinion as to the authenticity of the fourth Gospel. I do not think, however, that this change materially affects my main argument, and have therefore made no alteration in what I had written. I can see that I have fallen into some error by having started on a wrong assumption, but the assumption is one which many accept, and what I

have written seems to me to follow naturally from it.
Moreover, whether John wrote the fourth Gospel or no, I
think that Jesus Christ must have been seen alive after his
crucifixion, for Christianity could never have spread without the foundation of this supposed miracle; and of all the
accounts of his reappearance, none is to my mind so impressed with an air of probability as that given in the fourth
Gospel, no matter by whom that Gospel was written. Christ
alone as a crucified teacher was not enough for the rise of
Christianity: great as he was, more than this was wanted for
the enthusiasm which followed: but Christ, great in himself,
and by his supposed miraculous resurrection raised at once
into the region of the superhuman, would suffice for the
spread of the religion. Again, St. Paul's First Epistle to the
Corinthians is universally granted as the work of Paul; in
that Epistle he asserts the reappearance of Christ in the
most explicit terms. I cannot think it at all likely that he
should in a matter of this sort be mistaken. The first
teachers clearly said they had seen Christ alive after the
crucifixion. Paul's words leave no doubt on this head, and
the twelve were not likely to say they had seen Christ unless
they *had* seen him. All the writers agree that they were not
expecting to see him, and half the battle lies in this; so that I
can feel no doubt both on the ground of external evidence
and internal probability that Christ was actually seen alive.
Neither in my own mind do I doubt that the account of the
crucifixion and resurrection given in John's Gospel is really
derived from John himself even though John did not write
the Gospel. I should find it impossible to substantiate this by
argument, but it is not improbable that John told his version
of the story at Ephesus, and that the writer of the Gospel,
whatever end he may have had in writing it, should have
adhered to history where accuracy neither made nor mar-
ried his plan. I thought it better therefore to leave the
question of the authenticity of the fourth Gospel alone.

The Evidence for
The Resurrection of Jesus Christ

Waiving all question as to the authorship of the fourth gospel, and assuming that the account of the Resurrection therein given is virtually the work of John, we naturally turn first to that account when we try to form a distinct conception of the circumstances connected with the resurrection of Jesus Christ. We have reason to believe that John saw what he says he saw, and that in speaking of the disciple whom Jesus loved, he is alluding to himself. His account runs as follows:–

'The first day of the week cometh Mary Magdalene while it was yet dark unto the sepulchre, and seeth the stone taken away from the sepulchre. Then she runneth and cometh to Simon Peter and to the other disciple whom Jesus loved, and saith unto them, They have taken away the Lord out of the sepulchre and we know not where they have laid him. Peter therefore went forth and that other disciple and came to the sepulchre. So they both ran together, and the other disciple did outrun Peter, and came first to the sepulchre. And he stooping down and looking in, saw the linen clothes lying, yet went he not in. Then cometh Simon Peter following him and went into the sepulchre and seeth the linen clothes lie. And the napkin that was about his head not lying with the linen clothes, but wrapped together in a place by itself. Then went in also that other disciple, which came first to the sepulchre, and he saw and believed. For as yet they knew not the Scripture that he must rise from the dead. Then the disciples went away again to their own home. But Mary stood without at the sepulchre weeping; and as she wept she stooped down and looked into the sepulchre. And seeth two angels in white sitting, the one at the head, the other at the feet, where they body of Jesus had lain. And they say unto her, Woman, why weepest thou? She saith unto them, Because they have taken away my Lord and I know not where they have laid him.'

Then Mary sees Jesus himself but does not at first recognise him.

We must divide this record into two parts: firstly, we must examine what took place before John left the tomb; secondly, what happened afterwards.

I. It is clear that Mary had seen nothing miraculous when she came running to Peter and John. She had found the tomb empty when she came there. She had no knowledge as to where the body was, nor how long it had been removed. All she knew was that it was gone within thirty-six hours from the time when it was laid in the tomb; but how much earlier it had been gone, neither did she know nor shall we. Peter and John went to the tomb, and went right into it. They saw no angel – nothing in any way miraculous – simply the grave clothes (which were probably of white linen) lying in two separate places. Then, and not till then, do they appear to have had the first conception that Christ might have risen from the dead. Here for a moment we must pause. Had these men seen Lazarus raised from the corruption of the grave, and heard Christ prophecy that he should himself rise, or had they not? Had they for a space of two years seen miracle after miracle worked by Jesus Christ, or had they not? It is not believable that they had seen Lazarus raised and known of the prophecy that Christ himself should rise, and yet that they should not be in a state of inconceivably agitated excitement in expectation of its fulfilment. And this they were not. But it is very credible if Christ was seen alive after his crucifixion, and his reappearance was believed to be miraculous, that this one well substantiated fact should become the parent of all the other miracles and of the prophecies that he should rise. Thirty years in all probability elapsed between the reappearance of Christ and the earliest of the Gospels, thirty years of oral communication and spiritual enthusiasm, among an oriental people, in an unscientific age, in an age to which the notion of an interference with the modes of the universe from a point outside of itself was familiar from the cradle – an age which believed in anthropomorphic deity who had back parts which Moses was actually allowed to see through the hand of God which was hidden over his face – an age which, over and above all this, was at the time especially excited, being on the *qui vive* for a deliverer from the Roman yoke, and ready to follow almost any one who professed himself to be such a deliverer. Surely if the reappearance of Christ were once believed miraculous, it would not be wonderful that the prophecies and other miracles should be current within thirty years, among such a people and such times. *We* could not withstand such an incitement to let our wish be father to our thoughts. If we had been the especially favoured friend of one who died, and yet was not to be holden by death; no matter how carefully judicial we might be by nature, we should be blind to almost everything save the fact that we had once been the companions of an immortal. No one could withstand the intoxication of such an idea – not I nor the reader. A single miracle in the present day which we believed to be thoroughly substantiated would uproot the hedges of our caution: it would rob us of that notion of the continuity of nature to which our judgments are consciously or unconsciously anchored; but if we were very closely connected with it in our own persons we should feed on that idea, and on little else. Few of us realise to ourselves what happened so very long ago. We believe the Christian miracles though we should reject the notion of a modern miracle almost with ridicule; we should hardly even examine the evidence in its favour. The Christian miracles stand in our minds alone, and we conceive of them as so remote that we do not believe in them so fully as we ourselves imagine: we cannot judge from our belief in them of what the effect of contact with a miracle would be; we must look for this rather among modern alleged miracles – in the enthusiasm of the Irish and American revivals, where the influence of one mind excites another till strong men fall into hysterical tears like children: we must look for it in the effect produced by the supposed Irvingite miracles in those who believed in them, and in the miracles that followed the Port Royal miracle of the Holy Thorn. There never was a miracle solitary yet; a single one becomes the immediate parent of many; the minds of those who have realised a single miracle in connection with themselves become unhinged, and so deeply impressed are they with the intense importance of what they have known, that they become more powerful than those of men who have never been under such influences; their own deep conviction produces conviction on others, and so the belief strengthens till adverse influences check it, or till it has reached a pitch of almost grotesque horror as in the later Jansenist miracles. Surely then there is nothing extraordinary in the gradual development within thirty years of all the Christian miracles if the single one of the Resurrection of Jesus Christ were held to be well substantiated. But there would be something utterly foreign to all we know of human nature in the fact of men not anticipating that Christ should rise from the dead if they had already seen him raise another from death to life, and had heard him prophecy that he should himself rise again. Nothing can explain the universally recorded incredulity of the apostles as to the reappearance of Christ, save the fact that they had neither seen a single miracle, nor heard of any prophecy that Christ should rise.

I believe then that the facts recorded, John xx. 1-9, are in the main true. Mary found the tomb empty; alike unconscious of what had happened, and of what was approaching, she came to Peter and John simply to tell them of what had distressed herself, and of what she thought they ought to know. The two go to the tomb, and find every thing as Mary had said; when they are in the tomb it is not impossible that a wild dream of hope may have flashed upon their minds that the aspirations which they had so fondly nourished, were not to be all dispelled. Within an hour or two Christ is seen alive, and I cannot wonder if the years that intervened between the morning of the Resurrection, and the writing of John's Gospel, sufficed to make him believe that he had held a belief in the Resurrection of his Master, while he had still only wildly hoped it. This much at any rate is plain, that neither he nor Peter had as yet heard any clearly intelligible prophecy upon the subject: whatever *ex post facto* interpretation may have been given to some of the sayings of Jesus Christ, no saying was known to them which would of itself have suggested any such inference: we may justly doubt the scientific caution and accuracy of the principal actors, without even in our hearts impugning for one moment the honesty of their intentions. In conclusion then, the evidence as far as it came under John's own eyes amounts to this, that the tomb of Christ was empty while it was yet very early on the Sunday morning.

II. When Peter and John were gone, Mary stooping down, looked through her tears into the darkness of the tomb, and saw two angels clothed in white who asked her why she wept. We must remember the wide difference between believing what John tells us he saw himself, and what he tells us that Mary Magdalene saw. All we can say for certain is, that he believed that Mary Magdalene saw what she said she saw. Peter and John were men, they went into the tomb itself and saw no angel: they saw nothing but the graveclothes (probably of white linen) lying in two separate places within in. Mary was a woman – a woman whose parallel we must look for among Spanish or Italian women of the lower orders at the present day; she had, we are elsewhere told (whether truly or not), been but recently possessed with devils; she was now in a state of tearful excitement, and looking through her tears from light into comparative darkness. Is it possible not to remember what Peter and John *did* see when they were in the tomb? Is it possible not to surmise that Mary in good truth saw nothing more? She thought she saw more, but the excitement under which she would be labouring partly at the time, and still more after she had seen Christ (and before she had had time to tell her story), would distort her vision in the first instance and memory afterwards: the evidence of women of her class and under such influences is not to be relied on in a matter of such importance as a miracle: it is true we are told that the angels spoke to her, yet the speech was very short, and very little to the point; the angels simply ask her why she weeps – she just answers them as though it was the common question of common people, and then she turns away. I cannot believe this. To my mind it is more probable that Mary *did* see two white objects in the tomb, and that her imagination, thrown into fever by the reappearance of Christ, rendered her incapable of recollecting the exact facts of the case. I well know that my own imagination would run a great risk of being distorted under such circumstances, and I believe also so would the reader's. I believe that at the time or within a very short period afterwards, she believed that what she had seen was angels, and the development of the short and meaningless speech (possibly as much due to the eager, cross-questioning of others as to herself) is not surprising.

Before the Sunday of the Resurrection was over the case would stand thus: Jesus Christ, who was supposed to have been verily and indeed dead, was known to be alive again. He had been seen and heard to speak. He was seen by a body of men who had been already prepared to regard him as their leader, and whose previous education and tone of mind would lead them to an excess of faith in a miracle rather than of scepticism concerning its miraculous character. The apostles would be in no impartial mood when they saw that Christ was alive. The miracle was too near themselves – too fascinating in its supposed consequences for themselves, to allow them to go into curious questions as to the completeness of the evidence for the death itself. The Master whom they had loved and hoped in, was crucified and was alive again. Had either the reader or myself been born in that age, and known and loved Christ, these facts would suffice for *us*. The nature of our belief in our Master would be changed once and for ever, and so changed we undoubtedly find it.

Over and above the reappearance of Christ, there would also be a report current that Mary Magdalene had seen a vision of angels at the tomb in which Christ's body had been laid, and this, though a matter of small importance as compared with the other, concerns us nearly when we come to consider the narratives of the remaining evangelists.

Examine them we must. What was enough for those days is not enough for ours. I am not one of those who would refuse to believe a miracle if it were supported by such evidence as the bench of judges would at this day hold to be conclusive, but neither will I believe in any miracle however engrained into the creeds of the civilized world, merely because it was believed by 'unlettered fishermen' two thousand years ago. That the apostles did believe that Christ had risen from the dead is absolutely certain. They were sincere men, their lives prove this beyond all possibility of cavil. We know that they could have been guilty of no conscious fraud. But we also see that in the mere fact of Christ having been crucified, there was ample ground to make *them* believe that he had been dead, and that the notion of a miracle was not the same to them as it is to us. It was to them what it is now among the lower classes of the Irish, French, Spanish, or Italian peasants; a thing which was always more or less liable to happen, and which did not demand more than a *primâ facie* case in order to establish its credibility. If a man were crucified and seen alive afterwards, the almost instant conclusion would in those days be that he had risen from the dead; the almost instant conclusion among educated people now would be that he had never died. In those days men would ask evidence of the crucifixion and the reappearance; with the establishment of these two points they would be satisfied, at the present time this would not be enough, we should require the most ample testimony, that not only the appearance of death, but death itself had actually ensued on the crucifixion. We should also examine with the most critical minuteness all the circumstances connected with the reappearance of him whom we had supposed dead. We should enquire how long he had hung upon the cross, and what became of the body when it was taken down; unless the answers upon these points were such as to exclude even the remotest possiblity of life having remained, we should not hesitate for a moment in refusing to believe that the reappearance was miraculous. I am speaking of impartial examiners, of men who had no interest either in believing or rejecting; but I grant that even now, if our affections and our hopes for a glorious kingdom in a world beyond the grave were enlisted on the side of the miracle, it would go hard with the judicial candour of the greater portion of us: even more would it go hard if we believed that miracles were still occasionally worked in England, and that a few hundred years ago they had been much more signal and common: but such feelings should be resisted, they are neither right nor wise; it is no merit to believe on insufficient evidence: the man who voluntarily allows himself to do this through habit or fear, saps the foundations of his intellectual faculties. It is grossly immoral to violate one's inner sense of truth by assenting to that which though it may appear to be supported by much, is still not supported by enough; the man who can knowingly submit to such a derogation from the rights of his manhood, deserves the impairing of his mental eyesight which is sure to follow on such a course. If a good thing can be believed legitimately, let us believe it and be thankful, but if not we have no right to believe in it at all. I am not speaking against those who *do* believe in the miraculous character of Christ's Resurrection; I am well aware of the force of the arguments in their favour: I can see how overwhelming they must appear to many, and remember how overwhelming they once seemed to myself. But surely it is plain that if a man doubts, he ought to examine; that if he examines he ought to examine unflinchingly; and that if the result of his examination goes against his previous convictions, he should not shy like a startled horse, but should meet it and look it in the face like a man.

Let us now turn to the account of Luke.

'Now upon the first day of the week, very early in the morning, they came unto the sepulchre, bringing the spices which they had prepared, and certain others with them. And they found the stone rolled away from the sepulchre. And they entered in, and found not the body of the Lord Jesus. And it came to pass, as they were much perplexed thereabout, behold, two men stood by them in glittering garments: And as they were afraid and bowed down their faces to the earth, they said unto them, Why seek ye the living among the dead? He is not here, but is risen: remember how he spake unto you when he was yet in Galilee, Saying, the Son of man must be delivered into the hands of sinful men, and be crucified, and the third day rise again. And they remembered his words, And returned from the sepulchre, and told all these things unto the eleven, and to all the rest. It was Mary Magdalene, and Joanna, and Mary the mother of James, and other women that were with them, which told these things unto the apostles. And their words seemed to them as idle tales, and they believed them not. Then arose Peter, and ran unto the sepulchre; and stooping down, he beheld the linen clothes laid by themselves, and departed, wondering in himself at that which had come to pass.'

When we compare this account with John's, we are struck with the resemblances and the discrepancies. Luke and John both agree that Christ was seen alive after the crucifixion. Both agree that the tomb was found empty, very early on the Sunday morning (*i.e.* within thirty-six hours of the deposition from the cross), and neither affords us any clue whatsoever as to the time and manner of the removal of the body; but the angelic vision is by Luke placed in the van of the narrative, and Peter's going to the tomb is reported as having taken place in consequence of it. The angels instead of being seen by only one, are seen by many; the women are not represented as almost stolidly indifferent at the presence of supernatural beings, they are afraid and bow down their faces to the earth: instead of making an almost objectless enquiry, the angels have a definite purpose; they allude moreover to past prophecy, which the women at once *remember*. True the apostles a few verses lower appear to remember nothing of the sort; they regard the story of the women as mere idle tales, but that is of minor moment. What shall we say? Does it seem improbable that the simple facts as told by John, should before the time when Luke's Gospel was written, have assumed the form in which we here find them? To my mind no, and that too with no conscious fraud on the part of any one of those through whose mouths the story must have passed. In John we have an eye witness. When he tells us of what he saw, there is the visible impress of truth in his story. When he tells us of what Mary Magdalene said she saw, we see the myth in its earliest and crudest form: there is no attempt at circumstance in connection with it: it is given by an honest man, pure and simple, and abundant reason for suspecting its historical character is given along with it; reason which to our minds is sufficient for rejecting it, but which would naturally have no weight whatever with John's, or indeed with ours if we had been placed as John was placed. But surely it would not be long in such times before many a little embellishment was engrafted on to the original story; no one would mean to deceive, but we know how among uneducated enthusiastic persons the marvellous has a constant tendency to become more marvellous still, and as far as we can see, all the causes which bring this about were more strongly at work shortly after the time of Christ's reappearance, than they have been in any instance which we can call to mind. The main facts were that Christ's tomb was found empty on the Sunday morning, that Mary Magdalene had seen angels within it, and that shortly afterwards Christ was seen alive. Whether the angels were seen first or last, by one or many, appears at first sight to be of little moment, but we may be very sure that the story would not lose in the telling, and that the angelic vision would soon find its way into the most important place and receive such little circumstantial details as it appeared to stand most in need of; in fact the first christians would not have been men and woman at all unless this had been so; but they *were* men and women, and they unconsciously exaggerated; the only wonder is that they did not exaggerate more: for we must remember that even though the apostles themselves be supposed more faultless, more judicially unimpassioned, and less liable to inaccuracy than they probably were (being men), there could not but be some converts in the very earliest ages who would be of an inferior stamp. No matter how small a society is, there are bad in it as well as good – there was a Judas even in the twelve; but to use a less harsh expression, there would be incautious reporters in the church before long; visions and dreams would be vouchsafed to many: many a marvellous narrative may possibly be referable to this source: there is no trusting an age which is liable to give a supernatural interpretation to any extraordinary dream. It was when Peter had been fasting and was hungry that we are told he dreamed of eating unclean food. I would not lay stress on the accuracy of the writer of the Acts of the Apostles, and should hardly feel sure that Peter ever dreamed of the sheet let down from Heaven at all; he may or he may not have done so, but we know what fancies crowd upon us in dreams, and observe that when we lay stress on any particular thing that we have dreamt, the chances are a thousand or a hundred thousand to one that we go wrong. It is not the safest people who believe in such fancies, neither is there any end to what may come of it if an age once seriously confuses its sleeping and waking realities. In such an age then Luke may have said with a perfectly clear conscience that he had carefully sifted the truth of what he relates; but our own, being older and wiser than his, recognises a different standard of credibility. He would believe at once what we should reject at once; yet it is probable that he too had heard much which he rejected; he seems to have been dissatisfied with all the records of whose existence he was aware; the account which he gives is most likely to have been a very early one; it might well be not a week later than the facts themselves, only told in Galilee not at Jerusalem, so that I can see no reason for charging Luke even with credulity: a mind which is highly sceptical for its own age may seem slavishly credulous to the next; and Luke may have, perhaps not unjustly, almost prided himself on the scepticism and impartiality with which he had rejected other accounts which had reached him. He believed firmly all that he wrote, and very possibly he believed all the more firmly from knowing how much he disbelieved; those who pride themselves on accuracy generally are more firmly persuaded when they are misled at all than other people are: they are aware of the general bias of their minds and feel that their habitual caution gives them a right to hold strongly whatever they do hold; if then by an almost irresistible chain of causes their standard of caution is not quite high enough, we can expect nothing but a greater degree of confidence in proportion to the generally greater degree of scepticism.

Let us now turn to Mark. He writes thus:–

'And when the sabbath was past, Mary Magdalene, and Mary the mother of James, and Salome, had brought sweet spices, that they might come and anoint him. And very early in the morning the first day of the week, they came unto the sepulchre at the rising of the sun. And they said among themselves, Who shall roll us away the stone from the door of the sepulchre? And when they looked, they saw that the stone was rolled away: for it was very great. And entering into the sepulchre, they saw a young man sitting on the right side, clothed in a long white garment; and they were affrighted. And he saith unto them, Be not affrighted: Ye seek Jesus of Nazareth, which was crucified: he is risen, he is not here: behold the place where they laid him. But go your way, tell his disciples and Peter that he goeth before you into Galilee: there shall ye see him, as he said unto you. And they went out quickly, and fled from the sepulchre; for they trembled and were amazed: neither said they any thing to any man; for they were afraid. Now when Jesus was risen early the first day of the week, he appeared first to Mary Magdalene, out of whom he had cast seven devils. And she went and told them that had been with him, as they mourned and wept. And they, when they heard that he was alive, and had been seen of her, believed not.'

Here we have substantially the same version as we find in Luke: there is only one angel, but this is an inaccuracy which we would not lay stress upon; the vision is again placed in the van of the narrative, and the fear of the women is brought even more prominently forward. The angel reminds the women that Christ had said that he should be seen by his apostles in Galilee, of which saying we again see that the apostles have no recollection. The linen clothes have quite dropped out of the story, and we can detect no remnant of Peter and John's visit to the tomb unless a faint trace of it is to be seen in the command to tell *Peter* and the rest, that Christ was risen. We have the same substratum of facts, the tomb empty when the women came there, a report of angels seen within it, and the subsequent reappearance of Jesus Christ – but neither John, Luke, nor Mark afford us the slightest clue as to the time and manner of the removal of the body from the tomb; there is nothing in any of their narratives to preclude its having been taken away on the very night of the crucifixion itself. But Christ reappeared: his reappearance was conceived to be miraculous; Mary Magdalene said she had seen angels in the tomb – who would doubt her when so far greater a marvel than this was palpably manifest to all? Who would care to enquire very particularly whether there were two angels or only one? who would scrutinise the exact moment of their appearance, and what minutely accurate account of their words could be expected? Any speech that was tolerably plausible would have been accepted under the circumstances by both the reader and myself, and none will cavil at Mark for inaccuracy any more than at Luke. The amplification of the story was inevitable; the very candour of the writers in leaving so many loop-holes for escape from the miraculous, is proof (if proof were needed) of their sincerity; nevertheless it is also proof that they were each more or less inaccurate; and we have in the reappearance of Christ himself an abundant palliation for the amount of inaccuracy which we find. Given one great miracle, proved with a sufficiency of evidence for the proclivities and capacities of the age, and the rest is easy. This groundwork we have in the fact that Christ was crucified and was afterwards seen alive.

Let us now turn to Matthew. Here we find all changed. If his account is trustworthy we have the very thing which was wanted: we have the knowledge given us of the time and manner of the removal of the stone from the tomb. We find that it was not gone when the women came, but that it had been sealed and a guard set upon it. Let us read his version.

'Now the next day, that followed the day of the preparation, the chief priests and Pharisees came together unto Pilate, Saying, Sir, we remember that that deceiver said, while he was yet alive, After three days I will rise again. Command therefore that the sepulchre be made sure until the third day, lest his disciples come by night and steal him away, and say unto the people, He is risen from the dead: so the last error shall be worse than the first. Pilate said unto them, Ye have a watch: go your way, make it as sure as ye can. So they went, and made the sepulchre sure, sealing the stone, and setting a watch. In the end of the sabbath, as it began to dawn towards the first day of the week, came Mary Magdalene and the other Mary to see the sepulchre. And, behold, there was a great earthquake: for the angel of the Lord descended from heaven, and came and rolled back the stone from the door, and sat upon it. His countenance was like lightning, and his raiment white as snow: And for fear of him the keepers did shake, and became as dead men. And the angel answered and said unto the women, Fear not ye: for I know that ye seek Jesus, which was crucified. He is not here: for he is risen, as he said. Come, see the place where the Lord lay. And go quickly, and tell his disciples that he is risen from the dead; and, behold, he goeth before you into Galilee; there shall ye see him: lo, I have told you. And they departed quickly from the sepulchre with fear and great joy; and did run to bring his disciples word. And as they went to tell his disciples, Jesus met them, saying, All hail. And they came and held him by the feet, and worshipped him (*cf*. John xx. 16, 17). Then said Jesus unto them, Be not afraid: go tell my brethren that they go into Galilee, and there shall they see me. Now when they were going, behold, some of the watch came into the city, and shewed unto the chief priests all the things that were done. And when they were assembled with the elders, and had taken counsel, they gave large money unto the soldiers, saying, Say ye, His disciples came by night, and stole him away while we slept. And if this come to the governor's ears, we will persuade him and secure you. So they took the money, and did as they were taught: and this saying is commonly reported among the Jews until this day.'

The question arises how far is this narrative true, and how far is it exaggerated? That there is either exaggeration or omission somewhere is clear, for nothing can be plainer, according to the other three writers, than that the tomb was empty when it was first seen on the Sunday morning – of these three John was an eye witness and we can depend upon him; Luke we have every reason to suppose was the companion of St. Paul, and as careful a writer as the condition of the times would allow; but of Matthew we know positively nothing. Perhaps the simplest way of examining his narrative will be by way of commenting on Alford's notes upon the twenty-eighth chapter of St. Matthew's Gospel, and on his last note on the twenty-seventh.

Speaking of the independence of the four narratives (in his note on Matt. xxviii. 1-10) and referring to their 'minor discrepancies,' the dean says 'supposing us to be acquainted with every thing said and done in its order and exactness we should doubtless be able to reconcile or account for the present forms of the narratives; but not having this key to the harmonising of them, all attempts to do so in minute particulars must be full of arbitrary assumptions and carry no weight with them: and I may remark that of all the harmonies those of the incidents of these chapters are to me the most unsatisfactory. Giving their compilers all credit for the best intentions, I confess they seem to me to weaken instead of strengthening the evidence, which now rests (speaking merely objectively) on the unexceptionable testimony of three independent narrators, and one who besides was an eye witness of much that happened. If we are to compare the four and ask which is to be taken as most nearly reporting the exact words and incidents, on this there can, I think, be no doubt. On internal as well as external ground *that of John* takes the *highest place*, but not of course to the exclusion of those parts of the narrative which he *does not touch*.'

Surely the above is a very extraordinary note. The difficulty of the irreconcilable differences between the four narratives is not met or attempted to be met: the Dean seems to consider the attempt as hopeless: no one, according to him, has been as yet successful, neither can he see any prospect of succeeding better himself: the expedient therefore which he proposes is that the whole should be taken on trust, that it should be assumed that no discrepancy which could not be accounted for would be found if the facts were known in the exact order in which they occurred. In other words he ignores the difficulty. Yet the difficulty is a very grave one. A story so extraordinary that we should never believe it were it to be told us as having happened in our own times is given us by four different writers in four more or less different ways. The confusion in which the differences leave us is allowed to be so hopeless that any attempt to reconcile them leaves the matter worse than at first. We know that the age in which the accounts were written was credulous and unscientific, while three of the writers are unknown to have been personally concerned in what they tell us. These three deal most in the miraculous, while the fourth, whom we accept as an eye witness, writes in such a way as to suggest a simple explanation of the whole. Nevertheless, according to the Dean, we are to feel no doubt: by the simple process of passing over the difficulty our faith will remain unshaken.

Let us now turn to note on Matt. xxvii. 62-66.

With regard to the setting of the watch and the sealing of the stone, the Dean tells us that the narrative following (*i.e.* the account of the guard and the earthquake) 'has been much impugned and its historical accuracy very generally given up even by the best of the German commentators (Olshausen, Meyer; also De Wette, Hase, and others). The chief difficulties found in it seem to be: (1) How should the chief priests, etc., know of Christ's having said, in three days I will rise again, when the saying was hid even from his own disciples? The answer to this is easy. The *meaning* of the saying may have been and was, hid from the disciples; but the fact of its having been said could be no secret. Not to lay any stress on John ii. 19 ("Jesus answered and said unto them – destroy this temple and in three days I will build it up"), we have the direct prophecy of Matt. xii. 40 ("For as Jonah was in the whale's belly three days and three nights, so shall the Son of Man be in the heart of the earth three days and three nights"): besides this there would be a rumour current through the intercourse of the apostles with others that he had been in the habit of so saying. As to the understanding of the words we must remember that hatred is keener sighted than love; that the raising of Lazarus would show what sort of thing rising from the dead was to be; and the fulfilment of the Lord's announcement of His crucifixion, would naturally lead them to look further to what more he had announced. (2) How should the women who were solicitous about the removal of the stone not have been still more so about its being sealed and a guard set? The answer to this last has been given above – they were not aware of the circumstance because the guard was not set till the morning before. There would be no need of the application before the approach of the third day – it is only made for a watch, ἕως τῆς τρίτης ἡμέρας (ver. 64,) and it is not probable that the circumstances would transpire that night – certainly it seems not to have done so. (3) That Gamaliel was of the council, and if such a thing as this and its sequel had really happened, he need not have expressed himself doubtfully (Acts v. 39,) but would have been certain that this was from God. But first it does not necessarily follow that every member of the Sanhedrim was necessarily present, and applied to Pilate, or even had they done so that all bore a part in the act of xxviiii. 12 (the bribing of the guard to silence). One who like Joseph had not consented to the deed before – and we may safely say that there were others such – would naturally withdraw himself from further proceedings against the person of Jesus. (4) Had this been so the three other evangelists would not have passed over so important a testimony to the Resurrection. But surely we cannot argue in this way – for thus every important fact narrated by one evangelist alone must be rejected, *e.g.* (which stands in much the same relation), the satisfaction of Thomas, – and other such narrations. Till we know more about the circumstances under which, and the scope with which each gospel was compiled, all *à priori* arguments of this kind are good for nothing.'

It will be necessary to consider this defence of Matthew's accuracy against the objections of the German commentators.

I. The German commentators maintain that the chief priests are not likely to have known of any prophecy of Christ's resurrection when his own disciples had evidently heard of nothing to this effect. Alford answers.

1. They had heard the words but did not understand their meaning: hatred enabled the chief priests to see clearly what love did not reveal to the understanding of the apostles. True, according to Matthew, Christ had said that as Jonah was three days and three nights in the whale's belly

so the Son of Man should be three days and three nights in
the heart of the earth; but it would be only hatred which
would suggest the interpretation of so obscure a prophecy:
love would not be sufficiently keen-sighted to understand
it.

I answer firstly that if the apostles had seen Lazarus
raised when corruption had already set in, and had after
this ever heard any words capable of suggesting the idea
that Christ should himself rise – it is impossible that they
should not have expected the resurrection: secondly,
hatred is not keener sighted than love: thirdly, when
Matthew's accuracy is being impugned it is entirely beside
the mark to quote Matthew in support of that accuracy: if
Matthew in his version of the Resurrection be the inaccurate historian which the German commentators suppose, it
is equally possible that he may have been inaccurate in
recording the fact of the prophecy's having been uttered.

2. Alford says that the raising of Lazarus would show the
chief priests what sort of a thing the resurrection from the
dead was to be, and that the fulfilment of Christ's prophecy
concerning his crucifixion would naturally lead them to
look further to what else he had announced.

I answer. Firstly: if the raising of Lazarus showed the
chief priests what sort of a thing the resurrection was to be,
it would show the apostles also: secondly, that if the fulfilment of the prophecy of the crucifixion would lead the
chief priests to look further to the fulfilment of the
prophecy of the resurrection, so would it lead the apostles:
thirdly, that even Matthew does not represent the chief
priests as believing that Christ would rise and as attempting
to thwart a *bonâ fide* resurrection; he only represents them
as anxious to guard against fraud on the part of the
apostles.

II. The German commentators ask how was it possible
that the women who were solicitous about the removal of
the stone should not be still more so about its being sealed
and a guard set? If the German commentators have asked
their question in this shape, they have asked it badly and
Alford's answer is sufficient: they should have asked, how
the other three writers can all tell us that the stone was

already gone when the women got there, and yet Matthew's story be true? and how Matthew's story should be true without the other writers having known it? and how the other writers should have introduced matter contradictory of it, if they had known it to be true?

III. The German commentators say that in the Acts of the Apostles we find Gamaliel expressing himself as doubtful whether or no Christianity was of God, whereas had he known the facts related by Matthew he could have had no doubt at all. He must have *known* that Christianity was of God.

Alford answers that perhaps Gamaliel was not there. To which I would rejoin that though Gamaliel might have had no hand in the bribery supposing it to have taken place, it is inconceivable that such a story should not have reached him; the matter could never have been so quiet but that it must have leaked out. Men are not so utterly bad or so utterly foolish as Dean Alford seems to imply; and it by no means follows that because Gamaliel was not actually present when the guard were bribed that therefore he should be unaware of the circumstance.

IV. The German commentators argue from the silence of the other evangelists: Dean Alford replies by denying that this silence is any argument: I would answer firstly, that on a matter which the other three writers must have known to have been of such intense importance their silence is a conclusive argument of either their ignorance or their indolence as historians. Dean Alford has well substantiated the independence of the four narratives, he has well proved that John could never have seen the other gospels, and yet he supposes that John either did not know the facts related by Matthew, or thought it unnecessary to allude to them. Neither of these suppositions is tenable: but there would be nevertheless a shadow of ground for Dean Alford to stand upon if the other evangelists were simply silent: but why does he omit all notice of their introducing matter which is absolutely incompatible with Matthew's accuracy?

There is one other consideration which must suggest itself to the reader in connection with this story of the guard. It refers to the conduct of the chief priests and the soldiers themselves. The conduct assigned to the chief priests in bribing the guard to lie against one whom they must by this time have known to be under supernatural protection, is contrary to human nature. The chief priests (according to Matthew) knew that Christ had said he should rise: they did not believe that he *would* rise, but feared (so Matthew says) that the apostles would steal the body and pretend a resurrection: the motive assigned to them is natural, and believable enough, were it not contradicted by the narratives of the other three writers and the evident ignorance of any prophecy among the apostles themselves: but when we read of their bribing the guards to tell a lie under such circumstances as those which we are told had just occurred we say that such conduct is incredible: men are too great cowards to be capable of it. The same applies to the soldiers: they would never dare to run counter to an agency which had nearly killed them with fright on that very self-same morning. Let any man put himself in their position: let him remember that these soldiers were previously no enemies to Christ, nor as far as we can judge is it likely that they were a gang of well selected villains: but even if they were they would not have dared to act as Matthew says they acted. One word more will be enough: the discipline of the Roman army would never have permitted the bare possibility of such a thing being hushed up: the soldiers must have had an officer of some sort, and there can exist no question, but that had the events related in Matthew ever happened they would have been reported to Pilate, and investigated.

To my mind the reasons for rejecting the testimony of Matthew seem overwhelming; at the same time I do not feel that we should be justified in imputing to him any conscious fraud. Let him have written (whoever he was – for we know nothing about him) a little later or a little farther off, and the exaggerations might have easily come about. Christ was seen alive and angels had visited his tomb – it is by an easy transition that they visit it as soon as the women come, and speak to many, instead of being seen by only a weeping woman looking into the bottom of a tomb – and it is no very great addition to find that a single angel was actually seen to roll the stone from the door of the sepulchre itself. It must have been early objected by unbelievers that there was no evidence that the tomb had not been tampered with: and though the eager framer of the story of the guard (whoever he was) must be charged with pure invention, we cannot wonder that so desirable an addition to the completeness of the evidence of a miraculous resurrection should be early and easily accepted: twenty years would more than suffice for the rooting of the story, and as far as we can gather, Matthew's Gospel was then still unwritten.

We may perhaps take this opportunity to remark that of all the writers Matthew deals most largely in the marvellous and John the least. John is silent on the miraculous conception, the temptation in the wilderness (which can hardly be made room for in his Gospel at all), the transfiguration, the darkness and earthquake of the crucifixion and the ascension. We are compelled to believe with Dean Alford that John had never seen any of the other three Gospels, and that he had no design of supplementing them. Strange that the eye witness should be silent on so many of the most important miracles and that we should obtain our knowledge of them from those who were *not* eye witnesses – men of whom we *know* absolutely nothing. True John tells of some great miracles, and tells them with remarkable circumstantiality, but on the whole the miraculous element does not prevail in his gospel to anything like the extent which it does in those of the men who we have no reason to suppose ever were eye witnesses of any part of what they tell us. If John believed what we know he did believe as to the resurrection, it is no wonder that this belief should have distorted both his memory and his judicial faculty. He would believe much that he never would have believed otherwise, and hence (as I take it) the miracles which he does record. No man could stand against the pressure to which John's mind was subjected; neither is it surprising that the further we get from the known fountain head the more miracles we find. It would be inevitable, and no one should be dealt with harshly on account of it.

Let us as a commentary on the Christian miracles take the

following passage from Gibbon.

'The grave and learned Augustine whose understanding scarcely admits the excuse of credulity, has attested the innumerable prodigies which were worked in Africa by the relics of St. Stephen, and this marvellous narrative is inserted in the elaborate work of the 'City of God,' which the Bishop designed as a solid and immortal proof of the truth of Christianity. Augustine solemnly declares that he had selected those miracles only which had been publicly certified by persons who were either the objects or the spectators of the powers of the martyr. Many prodigies were omitted or forgotten and Hippo had been less favourably treated than the other cities of the Province: and yet the Bishop enumerates above seventy miracles of which three were resurrections from the dead in the space of two years and within the limits of his own diocese. If we enlarge our view to all the dioceses and all the saints of the Christian world, it will not be easy to calculate the fables and errors which issued from this inexhaustible source. But we may surely be allowed to observe that a miracle in that age of superstition and credulity lost its name and its merits, since it could scarcely be considered as a deviation from the ordinary and established laws of nature.' (Gibbon's Decline and Fall, chap. xxviii. end of §II. and near the end of the chapter itself).

Who believes these miracles? Yet on what better foundation do those of the New Testament rest?

Nevertheless as Dean Alford well says, the evidence as to the main fact of Christ's resurrection is absolutely unimpeachable. Christianity must have had a foundation, and the reappearance of Christ after he had been supposed dead is at once the best attested and the most credible foundation for it. It seems to me that the reappearance of Jesus Christ is as well attested as the assassination of Julius Cæsar. If Christ did not reappear, the very foundations of historical criticism are unsound: but I cannot think that there is any evidence worth the name for more than this, namely, that Christ was crucified and seen alive afterwards. Of his death there is absolutely no evidence at all. There is evidence that he was believed to have been dead, but there is no more; he was believed to have been dead by men who might have been easily deceived – by men whose minds were altogether in a different key with regard to the miraculous than ours are, and whom therefore we cannot fairly judge by any modern standard. We cannot judge *them*, but we can weigh the facts which they relate. Men's modes of thought concerning facts change, but the facts change not at all; in order then to get at the truth as nearly as possible we must turn to St. John's account of the crucifixion. Here we find that it was about twelve o'clock when Pilate brought out Christ for the last time: the dialogue that followed, the preparation for the crucifixion and the leading Christ outside the city to the spot where the crucifixion was to take place can hardly have occupied less than an hour. By six o'clock (so we gather from John) the body was entombed, so that the actual time during which Christ was upon the cross can be little more than about four hours. Say five – say six – say whatever the reader chooses, the crucifixion was avowedly too hurried for death in ordinary cases to ensue. The thieves had to be killed. Immediately after the crucifixion the body is delivered to friends. And within thirty-six hours afterwards it is seen alive again.

Would a modern jury believe that the death had been actual and complete? I cannot think it, unless there was brought forward such convincing testimony as to the actual death that there could be no possibility of doubt upon the subject. If Christ had had his head cut off, if he had been burnt, or even if modern medical testimony as to the completeness of the death had reached us, and yet within thirty-six hours he was again seen alive, walking, talking, and eating, there could be nothing for it but to admit the miracle: or, again, if his legs had been broken, or his feet pierced, and he was seen walking very shortly afterwards, we could say nothing; but what irreparable mischief is done to the body by the mere act of crucifixion? The feet were not always, nor perhaps (so Alford tells us, quoting from Justin Martyr) generally pierced, nor is there a particle of evidence to show that they were so in this instance. A man who is crucified dies from pure exhaustion: is it improbable that under these circumstances he might swoon away, and that every outward appearance of death might precede death itself even by some hours? Men have been left for dead, been buried for dead by their best friends – nay, they have been pronounced dead by physicians under circumstances where a mistake was far less likely to happen than at the hurried crucifixion of Jesus Christ. These reflections are surely very obvious. True the Roman soldiers thought that Christ was dead, and it is not likely that they should have been deceived. It is *not* likely that they should have been deceived, but it is even less likely that Jesus Christ, if he had been once really dead should have been seen alive again. It is not probable that a man judicially condemned to die should escape death, but on the other hand such cases have happened before now; and John – a most unexceptionable eye witness of what took place – tells us many things which would lead us to believe that what is not commonly probable might have easily happened in this case.

The crucifixion was hurried, the body was delivered at once to Joseph and Nicodemus, who, though they doubtless believed Christ to be dead when they received him from the cross, would neither in common humanity kill him when they found out their mistake, nor forfeit their high position by being known as the restorers of a condemned man. They would keep their own secret, certainly from the apostles, and probably, if they could, even from Christ himself. It is noticeable that we hear of them no more. Nevertheless, there arises the question, how far the spear-wound, recorded by John, is to be considered as necessarily fatal. Unless it can be distinctly proved that this spear-wound must have been fatal, it seems that the balance of probability would lie greatly in favour of Christ's having escaped death. If the spear-wound can be shown to have been necessarily fatal, the death of Christ is proved. The resurrection becomes supernatural; the ascension ceases to be marvellous; the miraculous conception, the temptation in the wilderness, anything and everything, becomes believable about one in whose case all human experience is found to fail; but the proof of the necessity of death's having ensued upon the infliction of this would must be as clear as daylight before we are justified in rejecting the natural solution of the mystery, and adopting the supernatural instead. And we must own, also, that once let Nicodemus and Joseph have kept their own counsel – and they had a great stake to lose if they did not keep it – once let the apostles believe that Christ's restoration to life was miraculous, and men's minds would become so unsettled, that in a very short time all the recognised and all the apocryphal miracles of Christ would pass current without a shadow of difficulty. This is the centre point of the whole. Let this be believed, and, considering the times, which it must be always remembered were, in respect of credulity, widely different to our own times, considering the previous hopes and expectations of the apostles, considering their education, Oriental modes of thought and speech, familiarity with the idea of miracles, and considering also the unquestionable force and greatness of Christ's character, with the really remarkable circumstances of the case, – I say, once let the resurrection be believed (and under these circumstances it is not remarkable that it *should* have been believed) and the rest is all explicable – the mystery of Christianity is solved. The question then turns upon the nature of the wound inflicted by the centurion. Can it be proved to have been necessarily fatal? Let us see what Dean Alford says upon this point.

In his note on John xix. 34, Alford writes: 'The lance must have penetrated deep, for the object was to ensure death' [the object is a matter of pure conjecture; the soldiers thought Christ to be already dead, or they would have broken his legs; what need then to kill a dead man? It may have been given to ensure death, and even in this case it may have failed; it may have been given in more wanton mockery of the dead king of the Jews; no one can say anything about it with even an approach to certainty from the evidence before us], 'and see John xx. 27.' [Dean Alford means to say that the wound must have been large enough for Thomas to get his hand into it, because Christ says, 'reach hither thine hand and thrust it into my side;' but surely words are not to be pressed in this way; I might as fairly myself press the earlier part of the same verse in a manner which would shock me to write as much as it would the reader to read.] 'Probably into the left side on account of the position of the soldier' [no one can arrive at the position of the soldier from the evidence before us, and no one would attempt to do so unless actuated by an almost nervous anxiety to direct the spear into the heart of Christ]: 'and of what followed' [the Dean here insinuates that the water must have come from the pericardium; yet in his next note we are led to infer that he rejects this supposition, inasmuch as the quantity of water would have been 'so small as to have scarcely been observed.' Is this fair manly argument?]

Here this note ends. The next begins upon the words, 'blood and water.'

'The spear,' he writes, 'perhaps pierced the pericardium or envelope of the heart' ['perhaps;' we cannot be satisfied with 'perhaps'] in which case a liquid answering the description of water may have' [*may* have] 'flowed with the blood, but the quantity would have been so small as scarcely to have been observed' [yet in the preceding note he has led us to suppose that he thinks the water 'probably' came from near the heart]. 'It is hardly possible that the separation of the blood into placenta and serum should so soon have taken place, or that if it had it should have been described by an observer as blood and water. It is more probable that the fact which is here so strongly testified was a consequence of the extreme exhaustion of the body of the Redeemer.' [If so, the death is not proved, neither the necessarily fatal character of the wound.] 'The medical opinions on the subject are very various and by no means satisfactory.' [In this case, when the medical opinions are 'very various and by no means satisfactory' (what does Dean Alford mean by 'satisfactory?') and when other circumstances attendant on the crucifixion are taken into consideration, and when the whole is coupled with the delivery to friends and the reappearance of the sufferer with the wounds on his body within thirty-six hours afterwards, a man may be very readily pardoned for refusing to believe that the wound was fatal.]

So stand the two first of Dean Alford's notes upon this subject. I feel that I have been led to speak with great severity concerning them, and yet I know not that I have used greater plainness than the nature of the case justifies. I firmly believe that Dean Alford is convinced that Jesus Christ *did* die; but I cannot help suspecting that he feels the actual external evidence to be hardly sufficiently strong, and that he has therefore attempted, half unconsciously, to use a style of argument which is unworthy of the end he has in view. Indeed, even in these notes he is more candid than Christians generally are. It must have been a great effort to admit so much about the uncertain nature of this wound as the Dean has done, but if I am not mistaken he has been unable in this instance to attain that perfect honesty, that true manliness of argument, which the intense importance of the subject demands; but let us proceed to his note on John xix. 35, that is to say, on John's emphatic assertion of the truth of what he is stating, an assertion which, to my mind as much as to the Dean's, is a sufficient guarantee of sincerity. The note stands thus: 'This emphatic affirmation of the fact seems to regard rather the whole incident than the mere outflowing of the blood and water. It was the object of John to show that the Lord's body was a *real body* [yes] and underwent *real death*. [I can see no ground for thinking that John mentions this blood and water as a proof of real death; I believe that it is mentioned to prove that the body was a real body, in opposition to the gnostic theories which had probably appeared before John wrote his Gospel.] And both these were shown by what took place: not so much by the phenomenon of the water and blood [*i.e.*, it is admitted that the mere fact of the water and blood having flowed is not *per se* proof of a necessarily fatal wound] as by the infliction of *such a wound* (italics mine) [*such a wound!* What a wound? What has Dean Alford made clear about the wound? We know absolutely nothing about the severity or intention of the wound, and it is mere conjecture and assumption to say that we do, unless it be shown that the issue of blood and water *prove* that death must have ensued, and this Dean Alford has just virtually admitted to be not shown], after which, *even if death had not taken place before*, (italics mine) [a suspicion then may be admitted that up to this time the death was not actual and complete?] *there could not by any possibility be life remaining.'*

What can we think of this? I am lost in wonderment that Dean Alford should suppose that such a style of argument could pass muster with any ordinarily intelligent person. He has made words upon the subject of the wound, but he must surely see that after all the matter stands exactly as John left it, namely, that immediately before the deposition of Christ from the cross the body was wounded, more severely or less severely, as the case may be, with the point of a spear, and that from this wound there flowed something (whatever it was) that is by the writer called blood and water. Yet his sentences on this being ended, without his having added one iota to our knowledge, the Dean gravely winds up by saying that 'after the infliction of *such* a wound, there could not by any possibility be life remaining.' That the wound was inflicted I cannot doubt, but neither can I refrain from speaking severely about such trifling as the Dean has attempted to pass off for argument; let the reader turn to the Dean's notes and verify my quotations for himself. I confess that it angers me to see so solemn a subject so treated. For either Christianity is the truth of truths – the one thing which in this world should surpass all others in the thoughts of all men, and besides which all else should be insignificant except as grouping themselves round it – or it is, as far as the miraculous element is concerned, a mistake, which should be exposed as soon as possible. There is no middle course. Either Christ was the Son of God, or he was not. If he was, his great Father forbid that we should shuffle in order to prove him so – that we should higgle for an inch of wound more or an inch less, and haggle for the root νυγ in the Greek word ἔνυξε. If the narrative be doubtful, let us admit that it is so, and take the consequences. To me it seems that the death of Christ is not necessarily inferred from the fact of his having been wounded, as recorded by St. John, and that in this case the shortness of the time during which he remained upon the cross, the immediate delivery of the supposed corpse to friends; and, above all, the subsequent reappearance of Christ himself with the wound still open upon his body – are ample justification for refusing to believe that he verily and indeed died upon the cross. There is nothing unreasonable in refusing credence upon these grounds, and it would surely appear a monstrous supposition to hold that any benevolent or intelligent God would have left a matter of such unutterable importance in a state of such miserable uncertainty, when the addition of so trifling an amount of evidence would have been sufficient to establish it beyond all reasonable controversy if it were actually true.

It is urged however that the resurrection does not stand alone and cannot be dealt with singly; it is said that the previous life and miracles of Christ must be taken into consideration. That the Old Testament prophecies and miracles are a part of the proof of Christianity – that the miracles of the apostles are proofs, that the ascension is a proof, and that though no one of these things can be proved *per se* yet they all help to prove each other. Thus I have known people assume the death and resurrection of Christ in order to prove the ascension, and then use the ascension to prove the death and resurrection. They use the other alleged miracles of Christ in order to prove the resurrection, and having proved the resurrection by this means they declare that all cavilling about the other miracles is mere captiousness and folly. I have known many people argue in this way: yet surely they would hardly contend that upon any other subject but Christianity their process of reasoning would be a fair one. They would not admit it in geometry or science in general. If one point is settled first, it may be fairly taken as a base of operations for further argument: but it is surely unfair to prove one disputed proposition by assuming another disputed proposition, and then to take the thing so proved in order to prove the assumption which proved it. It is for this reason that I ignore all the other miracles: I have been endeavouring to investigate the actual evidence which we possess for a certain fact: the other miracles are as much impugned as the resurrection, and it is therefore impossible to insist on them as proof at all.

It will, however, be advisable to devote a short space to the consideration of the ascension. This is so closely con-

nected with the resurrection that it is impossible not to feel a
desire to see whether the evidence may not be stronger here
than in the case of the resurrection; if it were I would grant
that a far less conclusive proof of the resurrection would at
any rate satisfy myself, but I think we shall find that the
ascension is worse substantiated than the resurrection.

John is utterly silent upon this subject. Paul in quoting the
last recorded appearances of his Master, in a passage where
a mention of Christ's ascent into heaven might be most
reasonably looked for, is also entirely silent (see 1 Cor. xv.
5-9). The last verses of Mark's Gospel are acknowledged to
be very doubtful, and even there the subject is dismissed in
a verse. Luke in his Gospel barely mentions the fact that
Christ was carried up to heaven, as though he knew none of
the details. In his subsequent work he gives us the only
account of the ascension which we have, the circumstances
having evidently come to his knowledge since he wrote his
Gospel. But how Luke got his knowledge we have no means
of ascertaining. That the belief of the very earliest ages of
the church was that Christ was at the right hand of God in
Heaven is indisputable; but no one who professes to have
seen him on his way thither has left us a word upon the
subject; and that John might have done so, had Luke's
account been true, is certain. It is also most inexplicable that
Luke should not have heard the circumstances attendant
upon the ascension at the time he wrote his Gospel. He
knew so much which was of far less importance, that his not
knowing these is strongly suggestive of the inference that
nobody else knew them; and there is little difficulty in
supposing that the particulars may have gradually been
revealed in night visions – or been communicated in one or
other of the many ways in which extraordinary circumstances *are* communicated – in the thirty years of enthusiasm
which elapsed between the supposed ascension of Christ
and the writing of Luke's second work: it is not surprising
that a firm belief in Christ's having survived death should
have established itself in consequence of the actual circumstances that followed upon the crucifixion. Is it then strange
that this should develope itself into the belief that Christ
was now in heaven sitting at the right hand of God the

Father? And finally, is it strange that a circumstantial account of the manner of his leaving this earth should in the course of time be still further revealed?

It will be seen in the above pages that I have rejected all idea of wilful fraud on the part of the first founders of Christianity. Joseph and Nicodemus probably knew the truth, but they were placed in a very difficult position; they had no intention of deceiving in the first instance, and could hardly help continuing to deceive if they had done what I suppose they did. I need not say with what satisfaction I retain my belief in the perfect sincerity of those who lived and died for the religion which they founded. It has been too common to suppose that there is no alternative between regarding the Apostles as almost superhuman beings or as consummate villains. To me it appears that if they be taken simply as honest but uneducated men, subjected to a very unusual course of exciting incidents in an enthusiastic age and country, we shall find that no fraud should be imputed to them, and that nothing less than the foundation of Christianity could well have come about. The Apostles are generally supposed to have been sceptical beyond all conceivable scepticism; their hearts were so steeled against belief that they would not be convinced by evidence more powerful if possible, than that of their own senses, but if I have realised to myself rightly the effect which a well-proved miracle would have upon such men as the Apostles in such times as those they lived in, I think I am justified in saying that the single supposed miracle of the resurrection is sufficient to account for all that followed.

Appendix

I WILL add a few words as to the other miracles recorded by John. What shall we say of the healing of the man who was born blind? of the feeding of the five thousand? the raising of Lazarus? Let us take the last as being the strongest ground for an opponent.

There are three positions which may be taken in regard to it:— Firstly, we may believe the miracle; secondly, we may suppose collusion; thirdly, we may reject the narrative as being either wholly fictitious, or an exaggeration of certain lost occurrences that were in reality less marvellous.

I. 1. I have already more than once pointed out how incredible it is that the Apostles should have seen Lazarus raised and heard Christ prophecy his own resurrection and yet be incredulous about that resurrection when it actually took place. The reader would, under such circumstances, have been on the tip-toe of expectation for the reappearance of his master; but as we learn from the unanimous testimony of all the Evangelists, the Apostles themselves expected nothing less.

2. The conduct assigned to the chief priests is incredible: that they should believe the fact and yet act in the manner stated by John is contrary to human nature. The supernatural has too great a hold on men's imagination to allow them deliberately to oppose it, if they believe it to be truly supernatural. Men are often obstinate, prejudiced, narrow-minded, cowardly, and so forth; but they are not capable of deliberately concerting a crime in the unblushing manner represented by John and Matthew. To take a somewhat weak example from modern times: who would

believe that the leading medical practitioners in London had called a meeting, and that the late Sir Benjamin Brodie, after admitting that wonderful cures had been effected by homœopathy, had proposed a combined attack on the homœopathic hospital? We can understand prejudice blinding him or any one else to the most obvious facts; we can understand a whole class being so blinded; but we revolt from the supposition of a body of men believing yet openly concerting an attack. It is because the leading physicians in London do *not* believe in homœopathy that they oppose it. Here, on the other hand, the chief priests and Pharisees do not dispute the facts: they admit them. Yet John tells us that in the light of day they set themselves to oppose a supernatural agency, in the reality of which they themselves believed. It is simply impossible.

3. The silence of the Evangelists is inexplicable on the supposition of their having known this miracle. They tell of no miracle which will compare with it in importance; next to the resurrection and ascension the raising of Lazarus stands out as the greatest of all the miracles. Is it believable that Luke, for instance, should tell us of a penny being found in a fish's mouth, and yet be silent here if he knew the facts? If Luke had known them, he, at any rate, would have told us. Is it credible that it should have happened without his having heard of it, when he had heard of so many other and far less wonderful occurrences, and when this was so singularly public and notorious a miracle?

It may be answered, that the miracle was so notorious that it needed no chronicling: no more, for that matter, could the feeding of the five thousand, the death, resurrection and ascension itself. Luke professes to be a full and accurate historian, and it seems much more natural to suppose that his silence is caused by ignorance than by either indolence or the feeling that his narrative would be superfluous. How does his preface run? 'Since many have taken in hand to draw up an account of the things that have been fulfilled among us, even as they delivered them to us who were from the beginning witnesses and ministers of the word, it seemed good to me also, having accurately traced everything to its source, to write in order unto thee, most excellent Theophilus, that thou mayst know the certainty of those things wherein thou hast been taught.'

II. If the difficulties above pointed out induce us to disbelieve that the Apostles ever even thought they saw Lazarus raised from the dead, we are relieved from discussing the question of whether there was any collusion between Christ and Lazarus himself. I do not for one moment believe that there was ever any collusion at all; but it is satisfactory to reflect that the same arguments that induce a disbelief in the fact narrated, induce also a disbelief even in the bare possibility of collusion.

III. If we disbelieve the story in toto, how shall we account for it having originated, and for the circumstantial manner in which it is told? We believe that one hand wrote the whole Gospel, with exception of a few doubtful passages, and possibly of the last chapter: we have already assumed that hand to be the hand of John: we have laid stress on the facilities which John had for accurate information: we have especially chosen him for our guide: over and above this, we have admitted that his integrity is above suspicion; what alternative then can remain but to believe what he tells us?

This alternative, and this only, remains: we may believe that John believed the story, but not that he saw it. He never tells us that he was there. Had he inserted a few words alluding to his own presence, or, much more, had he told us directly that he was there, we should have been sorely puzzled; but there is a wide difference between believing what John tells us he saw, and believing all that he tells us whether we know that he saw it or no. Let the reader again realise to himself John's position. If John, having seen that Christ could not be held by death, was to hear the story of the raising of Lazarus, would it appear incredible to him? To me it seems as though he would not hesitate about believing it for a moment. Which of us would not believe so beautiful a story if told of a once dear friend whom we now knew to be the Almighty? Should we cross-examine all the witnesses before we decided to which side the balance of probabilities would incline? No; we should believe any miracle almost without examination. Everything that we could remember in connection with such a friend would assume a new and exaggerated aspect. Things would be now deemed significant which, when they happened, were actually unnoticed; one would stimulate the memory of another, and each would welcome any additional information, no matter how wonderful it was, while none would dream of investigating as to its accuracy or error. The supposition that Christ rose from the dead was enough to upset any men. That supposition, as I take it, arose thus: It arose firstly, from the power and beauty of Christ's own character; secondly, from the fact that he lived in an age when the Messiah was daily expected; thirdly, from his being crucified, but under such peculiar circumstances, that though he was thought to be dead, he nevertheless escaped with life. Combine these three things together, and add also an excitable Oriental people familiarized with miracles by their own traditions and aspirations: if this ground work of facts be given, I can see no difficulty in accounting for the origin of all the other miracles recorded of Jesus Christ and his Apostles; but I cannot believe that the other miracles were true, and yet that the Apostles scouted the idea of Christ's having been seen alive by the women. Given a belief in the resurrection and the belief in the miracles affords no wonder; we know how stories get about – how soon any seed grows in a soil which is prepared to receive it; but the disbelief in the resurrection is incompatible with the historical character of the previous miracles, and more especially with that of the raising of Lazarus.

Appendix II

A Surgeon looks at the Crucifixion
by W.B. Primrose

Reprinted with permission from
The Hibbert Journal Vol. 47, No. 4 (1949).

THE historicity of the Fourth Gospel is still a matter for discussion, and this article cannot venture an opinion on that issue, yet there are certain pieces of information in the Johannine description of the Crucifixion which are of considerable interest in the light of modern medical experience. Modern surgery and the growing complex of knowledge gathered from practical studies of cardiac resuscitation[1] and anæsthesia may have a contribution to make to the interpretation of at least one part of the Gospel narrative. It is intended in this article to analyse the incident recorded in St. John xix. 34, 'Howbeit one of the soldiers with a spear pierced his side, and straightway there came out blood and water,' and to see what explanation follows from a consideration of the medical facts, since modern medicine enables us to view these matters from a new and objective angle.

Crucifixion as a punishment was borrowed from the Carthaginians by the Romans for use in dealing with criminals of non-Roman origin. Generally, slaves and the 'submerged tenth' were the victims, people in whom little or no

---

1. 'Cardiac Resuscitation,' W.B. Primrose, *Brit. Med. Jour.*, September 21, 1935, p.540.

interest by relatives or friends was, or could be, shown. Rome, while not actually legislating upon this procedure, observed certain usages in connection with crucifixion with are of importance.

The accounts of actual crucifixion vary greatly in their details, but judged from the anatomical and surgical point of view, the Romans seemed to have evolved a technically satisfactory convention for the infliction of this barbarous punishment. The efficiency of this technique was demonstrated whenever crucifixion took place on a large scale, as, for instance, in those cases following upon various Jewish uprisings. The original method of fixation to the cross had been by nailing: this method was retained but modified to the extent that the nails were no longer driven through the hands and feet, but between the bones of the forearm above the wrists and similarly above the ankles in the case of the legs. In the first case the change was adopted because the tissues of the hands often could not support the weight of a heavy body for any length of time without being torn through by the nails: in the second case, even as a surgical procedure, it is extraordinarily difficult to drive a nail through the foot unless it is supported below by some rigid body such as a block or sandbag. These are the principal reasons why accounts mention the use of ropes to hold the victims up on the crosses; the use of little seats; and much more commonly, the use of a central arm projecting from the middle of the upright of the cross (rhinosceros horn, Cicero) upon which the victim was straddled. These were all means of relieving the hands of the weight of the body.[1] The footrests were to allow of the nails being driven through the feet. The Roman convention eliminated all these difficulties and proved most efficient, this being a major consideration with the practical-minded administrators of Judæa. Any sentimental notion of providing the victim with any kind of comfort or of amelioration to his misery was foreign to the fundamental conception of crucifixion which was torture, barbaric in the extreme,

1. The late C.S. Jagger's realistic bronze rood in the chapel of the Society of the Sacred Mission, Kelham, embodies these features. *Vide, Liturgy and Society,* A.G. Hebert, Plate XV.

maintained as long as life lasted, which was often to the third day in the case of resistant subjects if left undisturbed.

It may be mentioned at this point that the actual injuries produced by nailing in this manner, while causing great pain at the time, especially at the wrists, were not in themselves of great importance. The wounds were rapidly made with sharp nails (blunt nails would never be of any use in penetrating soft tissues). The muscles in the localities mentioned have nearly all given place to tendons which are separated and not lacerated by the nails. Bones thus escaped injury, as did also the nerves and important blood vessels, owing to their anatomical distribution. Such wounds would ordinarily heal by 'second intention' as a certain amount of sepsis would be present in the process; and there might afterwards be little disability. It is the use of this convention that permitted the fulfilling of the prophecy that in the case of the Messiah, there would be no bones broken at his crucifixion. While dealing with gross surgical injury, another point may be mentioned and that is the 'breaking of the legs.'

In the ordinary process of crucifixion, however, the victims, if not claimed for burial, were left to die from exposure and exhaustion; their bodies might be disintegrated by natural conditions including birds of prey, and more particularly, by the packs of wild dogs which roamed the land at night. These would tear the bodies from the crosses and devour them. Death thus came rapidly to the victims. The efficiency of this method of disposal was one of the reasons why the sites of crucifixion had to be beyond the walls and well away from the city proper.

The attitude of the Jews to crucifixion was one of loathing.[2] When, therefore, it came to the day of preparation for the Sabbath, the Jews objected to crucifixions being prolonged beyond sunset as their Sabbath was thereby desecrated, even by the upstanding crosses. In such circumstances it was usual for the Jews to appeal to the authorities

2. The Jewish code, as instanced by the care with which flagellation was administered so that the victim might not be humiliated by uncontrolled movements of bowel or bladder in the sight of his fellows, contrasts strongly with the barbarity of crucifixion.

to bring the crucifixions to an end, and the appeal was usually granted, soldiers being detailed to go and break the legs of any victims still alive, which was usually the case. Far from being a concession to the victim as hastening death of itself, it was a device to prevent the victims from leaving the place were they were thrown when taken down from the crosses which were then removed, for with the night came the wild animals.

Crucifixion was preceded by scourging. The physical effects of scourging were of much greater importance in this drama than were those produced by the spectacular nailing to the cross. Scourging was carried out by two kinds of implement, the official flagrum and the birch of staves. The victim was stripped of clothing and scourged at the official whipping post to which he was secured *facing* the multitude. The scourging was mostly across the front of the body. The use of the flagrum, which was a whip-like instrument having three chains each with a metal button, produced extensive subcutaneous damage with much bruising, giving a bloated appearance to the body later on. The skin might be cut where it covered a subcutaneous bone. The important feature of this beating is the inflammatory reaction quickly set up by the body around these areas of damaged tissue. This leads to a considerable elevation of body temperature accompanied by a febrile sweat strongly charged with the ammoniacal substance known as urea which is normally excreted by the kidneys. It has been known for the sweat of torture to produce a fine down of crystals of this substance on the foreheads of victims before death. This inflammatory process is well advanced and is possibly at its height in six to eight hours after the scourging. Apart from this, there is some shock from the kinetic energy imparted by the flagrum, and this shock may be out of all proportion to the visible extent of the violence inflicted as is often seen in modern war casualties where a bullet is stopped by striking a bone. It is of interest to note that flagellation was carried out by the Jews according to Deuteronomic prescription whereby the number of strokes with a single lash was restricted to forty, two-thirds of which had to be across the back. In the case of the flagrum, thirteen strokes would be allowed. It is likely that some observance as to number of strokes was made in deference to this order, for the flagrum, if used excessively, might quickly produce collapse from shock and so interfere with the procession to the site of crucifixion.

The use of staves or birches in scourging produced quite different effects. Here, the immediate effect was the production of intense pain with remarkably little damage to tissues or organs, even where the abdomen was the part principally thrashed. There are sound anatomical and physiological reasons for this. There is, as a rule, no damage to abdominal viscera, otherwise, in the case under consideration, there would have been internal bleeding of such a nature that the writer of the Fourth Gospel could not have reported that 'water' was seen issuing from the spear-wound. The shock arising from the use of the staves is due to the severe pain inflicted and develops rapidly as 'primary surgical shock.' This, with care and comfort, would pass off in a few hours; otherwise, it would add its effect to that produced by the flagrum which develops later as 'secondary surgical shock' which is progressive and is so often dangerous to life.

The 'water' mentioned by John is the result of the nervous upset of the blood vessels locally due to the over-stimulating effect of the scourging by staves. Certain individuals are very sensitive to such stimulation and the capillary vessels supplying the underlying tissues and membranes become paralysed and so allow the blood *fluids* which they convey to escape, rendering the various tissues œdematous or waterlogged. Where a membrane lines a cavity as in the general abdominal cavity, the seepage of fluid from the vessels takes place into that cavity gravitating to its lowest part. The fluid exuded in this way is clear and of pale straw colour, the red cellular part of the blood being retained in the undamaged vascular system. This process of exudation increases rapidly for five or six hours and then slowly subsides as is well seen in the case of a knee-joint injured by a violent knock. In this time a considerable amount of blood fluid or serum can be exuded into the abdominal cavity floating the intestinal contents upwards.

According to the Gospel account, Christ collapsed about three o'clock in the afternoon, more than six hours after the scourging, within which time about two pints of fluid appear to have been exuded into the abdominal cavity.[1] In the average case this amount of fluid cannot be spared from the general circulation without producing weakness and collapse. It is knowledge of this fact which governs the technique of the withdrawal of blood for transfusion purposes, the quanitity being limited to one pint on any occasion. We may suppose that, with this in view, the spear-thrust was made somewhere on the lower and more protuberant part of the abdomen, probably on the left side. There would be an initial rush of 'water' which, for anatomical reasons, would quickly stop and it would be tinged with blood issuing from a small vessel opened by the spear. The vessels in this locality are all somewhat small, and with the very low blood-pressure prevailing at the time, one vessel would contribute only a streaking of redness to the outflowing 'water.' If this is what was seen, then the observer could only have been a *few feet away* from the Cross of Jesus, observing all things very intently.

Surgically, this penetrating wound of the abdomen is unimportant in itself as penetrating wounds in this region so often are: wounds of this kind tend to heal rapidly, and if there is no septic infection, this one would cease to attract attention in a day or two. Contrast this with the wound some six cms. long described and pictured as being on the right side of the chest, the wound into which Thomas could put his fingers in the post-Resurrection appearance described (John xx. 27). It may be suggested that this wound lay over the sixth rib approximately and was due to the splitting of the skin and tissues over it by the flagrum. This wound would take longer to heal. There appear to be sound surgical reasons for stating that this obvious wound could not be that produced by the spear, for a penetrating wound in this vicinity would certainly pierce the lung (presenting the signs peculiar to such injuries) with every chance of a fatal

1. Such a condition of dehydration resulting from the withdrawal of so much fluid from the general circulation is always accompanied by thirst. John xix. 28 reveals this symptom in the case of Christ.

outcome. Also, the chest is peculiarly unable to secrete fluid in the same way as can the abdomen under the influence of very strong stimulation such as thrashing, a very common form of punishment. We may therefore conclude that the wound presented to Thomas was not that caused by the spear-thrust.

The principal reasons have now been given why a physically normal person (as Christ appears to have been) should have become unable to drag his cross to Calvary. The primary surgical shock had, by this time, developed fully; and when it was further increased by the nailing to the cross and the setting up of the crucified body in the vertical position, the total shock was so increased that Jesus collapsed after six hours of crucifixion.[1]

Early collapse on the cross was most unusual, which accounts for Pilate's surprise when he heard the report of his centurion that Christ had died (Mark xv. 44). This brief survey of the wounds inflicted in the course of this particular crucifixion shows that there was at no time anything likely to produce so early a death. The actual nail-wounds were surgically trifling as compared with injuries generally from which recovery is the rule. There were no sequelæ from the spear-wound; and the other wounds, caused by the carrying of the cross on the right shoulder, the blow upon the side of the face, and the crown of thorns do not call for comment here. Christ did not have his legs broken and so was spared the shock attendant upon this injury. He was also removed from the cross – a procedure more painful than the crucifixion itself – under complete anæsthesia (since the spear-thrust elicited no active response to the pain), so that there was little additional shock from this

---

1. Such considerations lead us to suppose that Christ, in comparison with others suffering the same fate, was very susceptible to surgical shock, both primary and secondary. Such susceptibility bears no definite relation to bodily physique. The most robust may go down fatally under the acute depression of the circumstances. Josephus reports that he interceded with Titus for three of his acquaintances who had been crucified for some hours only, but two of them died upon removal from their crosses in spite of all the medical treatment that could be given them.

cause. Hæmorrhage from the various wounds was very limited.

To those present the appearance presented by Christ after his collapse suggested that death had taken place and there were no reasons for doubting it. It is, however, commonly known that the generally accepted appearances of death might not satisfy a medical jurist who would insist on evidence of completely arrested circulation, and we seem to be faced with the carefully recorded evidence that after the spear-thrust *some circulation was still present, since active bleeding and secretions generally stop with the cessation of the heart-beat which alone is death.*

Such conditions of low vitality are well known to the anæsthetist of to-day; further, the nervous mechanism by which such a low-grade circulation is maintained (often for a long time under toxic or other conditions of acute depression) is well understood.[2] It often requires close observation to detect its activity and to realise that life is being continued with the possibility of recovery once the threatening condition is removed. These medical considerations have, therefore, a direct bearing upon the accounts of the Resurrection.

With everyone satisfied that Christ had died when he collapsed, little further interest was shown by his enemies. His own friends and relatives could do little in their bewilderment: it would also appear that none of them had the influence or the means necessary to claim his body for orthodox Jewish burial; and burial, even of criminals, should take place on the day of the death. This situation was, of course, relieved by Joseph of Arimathæa who was able to approach Pilate directly and get permission to have the body removed for burial. This, and the procuring of the essentials for burial appear to have taken the best part of two hours, leaving very little time for the ritual before sunset – about six o'clock. The need for haste led to considerable shortening of the ritual when the body was removed from the cross. *The body was not washed* as it should have been, and there was no time to use the herbs and

1. 'Natural Safeguards in General Anæsthesia,' W.B. Primrose, *Lancet*, August 11, 1945.

bandages which kept them applied to the body. Instead, the shroud was spread with an ointment or paste of aloes and myrrh to 'cleanse' the material. The body was then laid on one half of the shroud, the other half being folded over the body from head to feet. In this condition Christ was conveyed on a litter to Joseph's own tomb, where John and the womenfolk saw the body deposited. They then departed to prepare for the burial which they fully expected to take place on the morning of the third day. Entombment allowed of this delay.

The weather conditions on this particular day were those usual for the time of year: warm and sunny during the day with very cold nights. The darkness that occurred in conjunction with a mild seismic disturbance does not appear to have been accompanied by stormy atmospheric conditions, in which case the air would become warm and sultry. From this we may suppose that Jesus, practically nude on the cross, did not lose much body heat during his state of shock and collapse. When, however, the body was placed in the much cooler tomb, the difference of temperature would soon show a vital loss of body heat. With the change of decubitus from the vertical to the horizontal, some recovery would be expected to take place and an early sign of this would be a rigor or shivering fit as the initial muscular effort to produce more body heat. In a person so very exhausted, this would take a little time. If such rigor did not take place before John and the womenfolk had left, it must have happened very soon after, and showed Joseph that Jesus was apparently not yet dead, and was in a state of incipient revival. Medical knowledge would lead us to suppose that Christ could not have spent any length of time in the tomb, certainly not much more than one hour; it would have been impossible for anyone in his condition to survive even a night in such a place covered only by a linen sheet.

If we allow ourselves to follow the conjectural reconstruction of events as set out for instance by Mr Robert Graves and by various other writers, we find ourselves with yet one more non-miraculous explanation of the Resurrection. But this is a matter on which each reader will wish to form his own convictions, or to hold yet more firmly those already received. Judged, however, by the purely medical evidence provided in the Gospel accounts, it would appear that such evidence is not sufficient to pronounce (in the light of modern medical knowledge) with absolute certainty that Jesus was actually dead when his body was removed from the cross. This may seem to be a negative conclusion, but it is of great importance in any interpretation of the Resurrection appearances.

Some supplementary evidence seems to be provided by a brief consideration of Paul Vignon's scientific analysis of the Holy Shroud of Turin (see Paul Vignon, *Le Linceul du Christ*, Paris, 1901).

This religious relic, only occasionally exhibited, shows, as it were, in the form of a photographic negative, the 'outline' of the body it covered, both back and front, in quite remarkable detail. When the shroud was photographed, the negatives revealed the images in positive and these appeared very much as Western art has pictured Christ since the eleventh or twelfth century.[1] The blood-stains on the shroud show quite clearly that the nail wounds were not through the hands and feet, but where we have already shown them on medical grounds to be. The wound on the right side of the chest is considered by Vignon *not* to be the spear-thrust. In this we have concurred, but upon more anatomical and surgical fact that he was in a position to use. As already mentioned, there would be very little blood or exudate from the actual spear wound at the enshrouding, and so no visible impression would be made by it upon the cloth. Vignor analyses the bloodstains and the image very carefully and shows that all have depended upon the fact that the body was not washed before being enshrouded. In this condition, with the sweat of torture heavily charged with urea that was still being produced owing to continued life, the latter substance, aided by the moist and warm atmospheric conditions, together with the inflamed condition of the body, evaporated in upwardly moving currents of air under the shroud where they proceeded to act

1. D. Talbot Rice, Dept. of Fine Art, Univ., Edinburgh (by correspondence).

upon the resinous matter of the aloes paste, and in such varying concentrations that a photographic image resulted in which the anatomical features are all *normally proportioned*. Any impression produced by direct contact with the shroud could not do this.

In view of the foregoing, it is possible to suggest that Jesus may not have died on the cross although he suffered the experience of dying, his higher faculties disappearing as vitality gradually failed to support them. The Resurrection followed some time later, a definite interval of time separating the two phenomena of 'death' and revival, the somatic activities having been maintained at a very low level from which recovery took place as soon as conditions came to favour this.

From the scientific point of view there is little of note to criticise in the accounts of the Crucifixion and the Resurrection, unless it is the want of detailed observation and precise meaning. Everyone concerned in this drama seems to have acted in a manner consistent with the experience of a great tragedy and a great mystery, a mystery which twentieth-century medical knowledge may venture to elucidate.

W.B. Primrose.